A Pea Called Mildred

Margot Sunderland

Illustrated by
Nicky Armstrong

Routledge
Taylor & Francis Group

LONDON AND NEW YORK

ONCE THERE WAS A PEA called Mildred. She was born in a pod, just like hundreds and hundreds of other peas.

But Mildred was not like hundreds and hundreds of other peas.

When Mildred realised that she was a pea, she was very unhappy. She wanted more from life than just to be a pea and to have happen to her what happens to peas.

And when Mildred heard what she was likely to be when she grew up, pea soup, a pea-souper fog or part of somebody's fish and chip supper, she grew sadder and sadder. She had heard about peanut butter too, and someone mentioned pea-brains. She didn't fancy becoming them either.

In fact, Mildred had lots and lots of *dreams* . . .

. . . dreams about doing very exciting things with her pea life.

But when Mildred told her father about her dreams, although he really listened, he said, "I'm sorry Mildred, you see, peas don't do anything else. Peas are just peas."

So Mildred tried talking to her dreams. "Go away dreams, I have no use for you. I am just a pea." Her dreams felt very glum. They decided to fade into the background until Mildred might need them again.

Then one day, Mildred was put in a big red lorry. It was driving to a supermarket. Her friend Greeny said, "Soon we will probably be in someone's salad or soup."

Well, Mildred had heard about salads. The thought of being in the middle of some soggy lettuce or being pushed around by a rock-hard radish was more than she could bear.

"Enough! Enough!" said Mildred to herself. "I will never be mushy!" So she waited until the lorry drove past a pretty little house with a nice looking garden. When no one was watching, she rolled herself off the lorry, and on to the front lawn. Yippee! Mildred felt very excited and free!

But then she started to feel terribly lonely. At least if she had
stayed on the lorry, she would have been part of something –
part of a salad, or part of a soup, or part of somebody's fish and
chip supper. All alone here in the garden she felt awfully not-
part-of-anything. Just as Mildred was about to give up –
"Well, that's it now. I guess some slug will come along and eat
me up" – she saw something very bright out of the corner of
her eye.

"Hello!" said some pretty flowers who had seen Mildred
looking at them. "Hello, who are you?" asked Mildred. "We
are sweet peas," they answered. "But how can you be?" said
Mildred. "*I* am a pea. Peas are all the same, little and round
and green, hundreds and hundreds of us all the very same. And
you are all different colours and shapes."

The flowers laughed. "Well, it's true sweet peas like us *are* all different colours and shapes. But although you green peas are the same colour and the same shape on the outside, there's nothing to stop you being very different on the inside!" Mildred thought and thought about this, and suddenly found herself missing her dreams very badly. She wanted them to come back. But she had to find them first.

After a bit of searching, up popped one of Mildred's most
fantastical dreams. It was all about opening a tea shop. Mildred
had always dreamt of opening a tea shop. But as soon as the
tea shop dream appeared, so her father's voice filled her head:
"Peas can't open tea shops. Peas can only be peas."

Then, to make matters worse, a nasty thought suddenly bullied
its way into Mildred's mind. It was all about green mush, and
being sat on and poked by some very mean and frightening
fish and chips. Mildred began to feel very glum.

But then something happened! Mildred suddenly remembered the sweet peas saying that although she *looked* like all the other green peas on the outside, she could be different. So Mildred took a big box of crayons and some paper which she found on the grass, and started to draw her dream. She drew a lovely little tea shop with pink and yellow striped walls, and tables that sang to you when you were feeling sad.

And she drew everyone having free Christmas crackers and
jelly and candyfloss (because Mildred liked Christmas crackers
and jelly and candyfloss). She drew a menu with everything
lovely on it - but *no* pea soup, and *no* peanut butter, and *no*
mushy peas. Then she drew some bouncy castles in the tea
shop garden, and a super-duper paddling pool with magic
talking bubbles in it.

Now it just happened that the man in the pretty little house with the nice looking garden gave money to good business ideas. And at that moment, he just happened to come out to mow his lawn. He saw Mildred's dream drawing, and said that it was the best drawing of a tea shop he had ever seen. Then he said if she found a building, he would help her to open her tea shop.

So Mildred went to Mugglesby and found a lovely building by the river. And Mildred opened her tea shop.

And all the children who came to the tea shop loved the singing tables and the bouncy castles. And they loved paddling in the pool with the magic talking bubbles.

Lots and lots of people came, because no pea had ever opened a tea shop before. And everyone enjoyed the free Christmas crackers, the jelly and the candyfloss (except a few of the grown-ups, who felt a bit sick!).

How glad Mildred was then to be a pea – a pea full of dreams.
A pea whose dreams had come true . . .